To

Robert & Rosemary,

Hope you enjoy!

Best wishes

Marianne

x ♡ x

A RAINBOW OF POEMS

A Rainbow of Poems has elements of different emotions and feelings – colours in words along with seasonal attributions and reflections of things and places both past and present.

ACKNOWLEDGEMENTS

My deepest thanks to everyone who encouraged me and believed in me.

Also thanks to the people at Arthur H. Stockwell Ltd, who made all this possible, making a fantasy become a reality.

A RAINBOW OF POEMS

An Emotional Journey

Marianne Dodson

ARTHUR H. STOCKWELL LTD
Torrs Park, Ilfracombe, Devon, EX34 8BA
Established 1898
www.ahstockwell.co.uk

British Library Cataloguing-in-Publication Data.
A catalogue record for this book is available
from the British Library.

To my dad,
who always said,
"In the end everything turns out right."

ISBN 978-0-7223-4832-1
Printed in Great Britain by
Arthur H. Stockwell Ltd
Torrs Park   Ilfracombe
Devon EX34 8BA

MIA, BALLERINA

Mia, little ballerina,
She dances under the twinkling night sky
And only appears at night
As she's very, very shy.
Swaying and swirling her little body around,
She almost floats above the ground,
Dancing on the tips of her dainty toes.
She stops suddenly
For a little pose,
Her white fluffy tutu
Fluttering in the warm night air,
Her little tiara
Sparkling in her hair.
She blows a kiss to the moon
And makes a wish upon a star.
Mia, ballerina, dancer of the night,
She will soon fall asleep
In her secret place
By morning light.

MOLLY THE WITCH

Molly is a young little witch.
She has much to learn as yesterday
She crashed her broomstick into a ditch.
Molly has a little cat called Ming,
Who goes everywhere with her and loves to sing.
Today Molly has decided to study her spell book.
Ming gives her a loving little look.
Off they go to see if they can magic up something grand
And hopefully learn to fly and land.
Molly studied so hard all day
She forgot to make time to play.
A tired little witch and a sleepy little Ming
And two rumbling tummies making such a din.
"Time for some tea," said Molly to Ming,
And Ming looked up at her and began to sing.

LITTLE MOUSE

Little mouse,
You'd better watch out –
That naughty cat
Henry's about.
He will sniff you out,
Chase you and spin you
Around and around.
Little mouse,
I know you're only
Minding your own business
And looking to see
If there's anything nice to eat,
But mind you don't
Bump into Henry
Because he sees you
As a big sweet
When you sit and look up at him
By his big furry feet.
Far better to hide and be still
And wait for the all-clear
When that crafty cat
Henry is near.

PEGGY SPIDER

Peggy Spider,
There you are again –
Running across the living room
As fast as your little spindly
Eight legs can go;
And then run back
Into your cosy little hole in the wall,
Where it's dark and warm
And away from light and harm.
You think you're invisible
When you suddenly become still,
But I see you, Peggy Spider,
Under the curtain frill.
Know this to be true, Peggy Spider –
I really don't mind
Sharing my home with you
And I'll never harm you
As to hurt a spider
Is to hurt a friend.
Oh, and, Peggy Spider,
Spin me a pretty web
Before you scuttle off to bed.

PRETTY BUTTERFLY

Pretty butterfly,
I saw you float down
From the sky.
It's very kind of you
To come sit by my side.
I felt a bit sad and lonely,
And for a while I cried.
I see you have
Such beautiful wings
As you make yourself comfortable
On my little swing –
All the colours of a rainbow.
Pretty butterfly,
Where do you go
At the end of the day?
Are you a secret angel
That flies away to pray?
I hope you can stay awhile.
I'm sure I saw you smile.
Then you flutter around
In circles and all over the place,
Then gently land and kiss
My tear-stained face
And look at me
With your little angel eyes
As you flutter away,
Back up into the sky.
I'm sure you gave me a little wave
And whispered softly,
"Goodbye."

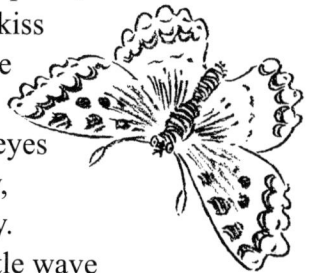

PUSSYCAT, PUSSYCAT

Pussycat, pussycat,
Come sit on my lap –
Let me look at your pretty face
Now the day's over
And there's nothing left to chase.
Silky long whiskers
And a cute button nose –
How I love to watch you pose!
Let me stroke your velvet fur,
Tickle your chin and ears
And listen to you purr.
Let me look into your big green eyes
And maybe see a nice surprise.
A wonder you are, so graceful and smart –
I hope that we may never part.
I watch you flick and wiggle
Your sleek tail side to side
As we play your favourite game
Of peek-a-boo and hide.
But now I see you getting sleepy,
Your furry head becoming droopy.
Off to bed we go
And find your little blanket and throw.
We'll soon have warm little toes
And sleepy eyes –
Soon they'll close.
Another day has been and gone.
Night night,
My precious little one.

SUMMER DAYS

Azure blue skies and fluffy white clouds
Go sailing by,
The sun is shining,
The birds are singing,
Busy bees collecting their pollen,
Butterflies fluttering
All around the garden,
Flowers revealing all their beauty
Like little soldiers
Performing their duties,
The sound of the lawnmower
In the far distance,
The ice-cream van's music
So persistent,
Ice lollies, cream teas and pink lemonade –
All a part of summer's facade.
Children playing in the park,
Little doggies run and bark,
Paddling pools and barbecues,
Funfairs and merry-go-rounds –
Such a happy sound –
The smell of daisies, buttercups and clover.
The summer days will soon be over,
And as the sound of the church bells chime
A distant memory of a happy time.

CLOUDS

Clouds in the sky
Sail silently by,
Fluffy, baby-pink,
Like balls of cotton wool.
Funny-shaped clouds:
Little white poodles and snails,
Dragons and feathers
And humpback whales,
Teapots and raspberry iced buns;
Clouds of lemon angels on horseback,
Little elephants
And lilac and blue cats,
Silver-grey cigar shapes;
Clouds bunched together
Like little grapes;
Flying-saucer clouds;
Orange and yellow
Top-hat clouds
And marshmallows;
Stormy clouds,
Inky blues and charcoals;
Dark eye-of-a-storm cloud,
Rumbling, angry and loud;
Clouds with sparkling silver linings
Like strings of diamonds
Floating along.
Tomorrow's weather forecast says,
'Clear bright-blue skies'.
No clouds – they're all gone –
But they'll be back someday
And I'll be glad
To see them again.

COLOURS

A bucket of blue,
A cup of cream,
A saucer of yellow,
A teaspoon of white,
A splash of orange,
A shot of red,
A dollop of green,
A ribbon of pink,
A band of purple,
A swirl of indigo,
A pinch of violet,
A sprinkle of silver,
A circle of gold –
A world of shapes and colours.

THIRTEEN SHADES OF LIPSTICK

I'm so lucky
I have somewhere to go
Each and every day
And a lipstick to match
In every way.
On Monday I go for a walk in the park,
So I'll wear my lipstick Barely Dark
And wave to the nice man
In his little green van.
On Tuesday I'm out to dinner –
I can't wait to wear my lipstick
Sticky Toffee Shimmer.
This Wednesday I'm a birthday girl;
As it's a special day
I'll be wearing my favourite lipstick, Apricot Pearl.
On Thursday it's meet the girls
For a coffee morning –
I think I'll put on my lipstick Amber Leaves Falling.
Friday I go and do the weekly shop
And I always like to look my best;
I must put on my new lipstick Coral Crest.
Saturday I will be at the skating rink,
So I'll wear my pretty lipstick Sparkly Pink.
On Sunday I will be at church
Meeting the new handsome vicar;
I'll most definitely slick on
My Rosy Pink lipstick a bit thicker.
Every Valentine's Day
I get my usual card and flowers

And bask in the loving haze –
I shall wear my lipstick Cherry Daze.
At Easter time I buy some lovely chocolates and caramels
Laced with a hint of honey –
I always wear my lipstick Pink Bunny.
Summer holidays are just around the corner
And I'll be in my rainbow-coloured bikini
With crystal-studded flip-flops on the beach
And wear my beautiful lipstick Gemstone Reef.
On Christmas Eve and there's magic in the air
I'll be wearing my lipstick
Golden Angel Hair.
Christmas Day – must get up early, jump out of bed,
Put on my best dress
And wear my lipstick Robin Red.
New Year's Eve and New Year's Day –
With the best of the excitement
Nearly out of the way
I'll be wearing my lipstick Rum Sway.

THE SEA

Colours of blues and greens
And shimmering creams,
Waves of sea spray
And frothy white foam,
Glassy beads of shingly stones,
Candyfloss-pink sands
And rainbow-coloured seashells
Adorn the land,
Minty-hued rock pools
Of hidden little treasures,
Sea-polished pebbles
Of all different measures,
Seaweed and driftwood
Alongside together.
Sea lavender and rock rose
Scent the air for ever,
The sea breeze sighing,
The seagulls crying,
Flying high above the mossy-covered rocks,
A young girl gazing at the sea,
The wind in her golden locks.

A DAY AT THE SEASIDE

A walk along the sandy beach –
Lots of seabirds,
How they screech!
The changing colours of the sea,
The sound of the waves –
How they soothe and caress me!
Little children with buckets and spades,
Boys and girls playing silly ball games,
Pretty ladies in bright summer dresses,
Sun hats and jewelled flip-flops,
Ice creams and soda pops.
People sunbathing
On the sparkly sand,
Taking in the views
Across the beautiful land.
Candy-coloured beach huts
And little sailing boats,
Surfers and people on pedaloes,
Pretty-coloured parasols
All in neat little rows.
Where the sky meets the sea
I carry my seaside memories
Along with me.

WAVES

Deep metallic blues –
The waves of the ocean,
Pewter-coloured waves of emotion,
A constant rhythm
Like a heartbeat.
Dark-grey waves of sadness,
Nervous energy sweeping over
And through your body.
Dove-grey and vanilla-cream
Waves in the evening sky.
Waves of clear salty tears
In your eyes.
Stormy-purple waves in your heart,
A feeling of longing
And a love that fell apart.
Waves of memories shuffling around
Like a pack of cards.
Waves of colours swirling
All around you.
Waves in your pretty long hair.
Waves of music
In the air.

THE SUNSET

A sea of colours,
Of blues and greens,
Orange and pinks,
And lemon and creams.
A lovers' walk –
A time to talk.
A day to remember
Of the things that we've done.
We're put under the spell
Of the evening sun.
We make a wish
And look to the sky,
Where the angels meet
And sprinkle their glitter
As the sun bows
And makes its last curtsies.
In the blink of an eye
It sinks from the sky –
Another day has been and gone,
A memory, an everlasting song.

THE WIND

A choir of whistling,
Howling and crying winds,
A sad old song of lonely hearts,
A love gone wrong
And torn apart
Telling a story
Of another place and time.
The trees all rustling in rhyme,
A fierce frantic wind at sea,
Of a lost soul
In its angry growl.
A warm gentle wind
That swirls around you
And tickles your chin.
The wind it breathes life
Into every corner and space,
Circling our world
In an everlasting race;
And as the wind god sighs
And whispers his goodbyes
It has soothed our hearts
And freed our minds.

THE PIANO

The piano waits silently
In the music room,
Polished so much
Its dark wood
A beautiful bloom.
It's very sleek and grand
And will soon be played
By loving little hands.
A lovely tinkling flowing sound
The ebony and ivory piano keys make
When gently pressed down.
A vase of flowers graces
The top of the piano,
A picture beside it
Of a little girl.
Her dress is yellow.
The piano has had
Many homes in its past,
But for a while it stood alone,
Forgotten and covered in dust.
A new home at last
Where it will be loved,
Adored and looked after,
Its sadness now
All in its past.

THE FAIRGROUND

The funfair has come to town,
Bringing with it gaiety and charm.
Crowds of people stroll around –
Lots to see and do in the fairground.
The smell of sizzling hot dogs
And the sweet, sticky scent of candyfloss
All coming from the little food van
Surrounded by hungry little hands.
Toffee apples and candy canes,
Loud music and silly games,
Ghost-train rides and the love tunnel
To go kiss and cuddle,
Merry-go-rounds and rides on bumper cars
Only a pound.
There's lots of people on the big wheel –
As it starts to turn you can hear their squeals.
Pretty fairy lights and sounds of happiness
Fill the warm, dark night air.
Wish it could last forever –
You never know, it really just might!

THE TEA PARTY

Nothing is as much fun
As a tea party in the summer sun:
Pretty girls in ditsy print dresses,
Their long hair such beautiful tresses,
Cucumber sandwiches and strawberry scones,
Fruit and jelly and sticky buns,
Paper plates and rainbow-coloured glasses,
Pretty napkins and bunting that matches.
Now the tea-party games begin:
Hide and seek and I spy,
The sound of happiness in their cries.
As the tea party draws to a close,
Warm little bodies and sore little toes –
A lovely day was had indeed –
Soon sleepyheads will proceed.

THE SWEET SHOP

The sweet shop stands on a little street corner –
It belongs to a nice lady called Miss Lorna.
Behind the shop's door another world
Of vanilla spice and sugar mice,
Multicoloured sweets in large glass jars,
Hundreds and thousands on little chocolate bars,
Barley sugar and nougat,
Chocolate raisins dipped in yogurt,
Jelly beans and vanilla creams,
Pear drops and lollipops,
Sugared almonds and Turkish delight –
Oh, what a wonderful sight!
The constant ching of the doorbell's ring
As streams of customers rush in.
Gazing at all the sweet splendour
Whilst contemplating their needs
Is making them week at the knees.
All a-hush now as the shopkeeper
Trickles the sweets on to the weighing scales,
Then bagging them with a little twirl.
The push-button till, it pings open
As money passes busy hands,
Then slams shut with a little twang.
Polished wooden floorboards creak and squeak
As the customers scuttle along
In the queue as they speak;
And as the last customer leaves the shop,
The flustered shopkeeper feels ready to flop.
A busy day indeed it's been –
Enough to put her head in a spin.
The shopkeeper puts the 'Closed' sign up on the door –
"Enough said, I am serving no more!"

SO MUCH TO DO

Why is there so much to do?
Day in, day out,
So much running about!
Peel the veg, cook the dinner –
Think I might just be on to a winner.
Hang out the washing on the line –
If I'm lucky
I might just have time
For a nice cool glass of wine.
Do the ironing, make the beds.
Now the family
Have been watered and fed,
Tie myself to the kitchen sink –
A few moments of quietness
And a chance to think.
Wash all the dirty crocks and pots.
I'm so achy,
My body in knots –
I've cut the grass and dug the garden,
Trimmed the hedges
And cleaned the windows
And the ledges,
Scrubbed the floors
And wiped the doors.
In my last life

What did I do
To deserve this all!
Now run around with the Hoover –
I'll be glad when the day is over.
Bedtime at last,
And I'm so tired
That sleep will come fast.
Sighs of relief
At the work I have done
Soon turn to despair and gloom
For in only a few hours
A new day begins
And some of the jobs
That were done today
Will be waiting there tomorrow
And the next day.

A BAD DAY

So you had a bad day –
It rained and the clouds
Were the colours of mud and grey.
Your hair's a mess
And there's a hole
In your best dress.
The washing machine is broken.
You had a fight with your boyfriend
And angry words were spoken.
You burnt the dinner
And the lottery ticket's no winner.
But hey, there's rainbows
Coming along the way
And your hair it'll look
Better the next day.
It was time to buy
A new bestest dress anyway
And a shiny new washing machine
In buttermilk cream.
The fight you had with your boyfriend –
Kiss and make up
Over a nice pot of tea
In a china cup.
It doesn't matter not winning the lottery –
You're lucky in so many other ways.
You've just got to smile
And muddle though the bad days.

WASHING LINE

Washing line –
There you stay,
Come rain or shine.
Candy-coloured pegs
And underwear with pink bows
All in neat little rows.
Dresses that look like ballerinas
In long tutus.
Stockings and suspenders –
Woo woo woo!
Skirts and shirts,
Trousers and ties –
Invisible people live in them,
I swear I tell you no lies.
You'd better peg them down well
Or it'll be bye-byes.
See the washing line
Turn into a spinning wheel –
It's spinning so fast,
A kaleidoscope of colours.
They'll all be dry at last.
The invisible people
Will all be gone –
The washing line bare,
But not for long.

HOW LUCKY WE ARE!

How lucky we are
If we wake up in our cosy beds
With no worries or troubles to be said!
How lucky we are
If we have our health and mind,
If we can see and not be blind!
How lucky we are
To have food on our plate
And not to worry if we are early or late!
How lucky we are
If we are loved and adored
And not be hated and ignored!
How lucky we are
To be on this beautiful earth
And to celebrate our birth!
But the clock is ticking
And we know it may not last.
Just like the dinosaurs
One day we'll all be fragments
Of the past.

IF I WAS

If I was a tree
I would rustle my leaves
As loud as I could be,
And if I was a flower
I would be so bright
And sparkly in the light.
If I was a little bird
I would sing my favourite songs
And from a far distance
Still be heard.
If I was a butterfly
I would dance upon the flowers
And fly so high
I could touch the fluffy clouds
In the sky.

WHEN NIGHT-TIME COMES

When night-time comes
There's a silence
And a gentle hum.
At the end of the day
The stars come out to play,
The sound of moth wings
Softly flapping by.
The blackbird's song so lovely,
Bringing a tear to your eye.
I see the moon gliding
Ever high in the sky.
Another day gone – goodbye.
I pull my soft knitted blanket
Up over my sleepy head
And dream my cares away.
When night-time comes
There's a silence
And only a gentle
Beat of a drum.

THE KISS

I waited all year
To give you a kiss –
A moment in time,
A second of bliss.
I still was not sure
To give you a kiss,
And when I did
It was a bit hit-and-miss.
I was scared to give you a kiss,
But it had been on my list
Of things I must do.
I so wanted to kiss you,
Though I was not sure
If I liked you or not.
It took time
And the courage I got
To give you that one
Very special kiss.

THINKING OF YOU

I think of you
Every now and then
When I'm pottering around
Having some quiet time
And making do and mend –
Friends made on holiday
That I'll never see again,
People just giving me
A friendly nod and a smile.
I think of you all
For a while.
Someone I helped
In times of trouble
And I put back together
Their broken bubble –
I think of them
Especially often.
Some precious things
That I've lost and found
Along the way –
I'll think of them all
Forever and a day.

YOU CAME ALONG

You came along
When I needed someone,
A friend to talk to,
Someone to lean on.
The friendship became love
Sent from heaven above,
But the colours grey and blue came along
And I realised that I did wrong.
I've done the tears and the time
For my forbidden crime;
Now I must let go,
Smile and carry on.
So it's goodbye and take care
For I no longer
Want or need you there.

THAT PLACE WHERE WE MEET

Every now and then
There's a place where we meet,
Secluded and quiet,
Away from the dust
And noise from the street –
A lovely park over the way
With nice seats and benches
To sit and relax on
All through the day.
There's pastel-coloured wild flowers
And seed heads floating
Up to the clouds in the sky,
Little birds singing,
In the distance a seabird's cry.
We sit in the car
And admire the views,
Kiss and cuddle
To banish the blues
Because our time is precious,
Our lives complicated
And in a muddle.
Every now and then
There's a place where we meet –
A secret corner in the world
Where for a few moments
Life is very sweet.

DOES IT MATTER?

Does it matter
If we're tall or short,
If we're large or thin,
If we're beautiful or ugly?
The beauty lies within.
Does it matter
If the colour of our skin
Is pale or dark,
Yellow, red or even green?
We're all under the same blue sky.
Does it matter
If we're clever
Or not so bright?
It's knowing the difference
Between wrong and right.
Does it matter
What religion we are?
We all came from
The sun and the stars.
Does it matter
If we don't speak
The same words as each other?
We all see the same face
Of the moon in the sky.
Does it matter
If we're rich or poor?
An angel will still
Come to our door.

ANOTHER YOU, ANOTHER ME

Is there another blue world, another universe,
A gateway to another time and place?
Are there other people out there,
All with a friendly smile upon their face,
Another you, another me?
On these other worlds
Are there pink trees and rainbow-coloured flowers
And animals with special powers,
Another you, another me?
On other worlds
Is there no pollution,
No wars to fight?
Is there a day and a night,
Another you, another me?

WHEN TOMORROW COMES

Will I still be here
When tomorrow comes?
Will my heart still beat
Like a gentle drum?
Will the birds still sing
And the sky be blue?
Will I still be
In love with you?
When tomorrow comes
Will my life be complete
Or will I fall into a messy heap?
Will the world still be turning
And my mind still a-whirling?
When tomorrow comes
Will it be a perfect day
Or end in tears, sadness and dismay?
The wait is long
And feelings ever strong.
I'll be brave and scared,
My soul completely bared
When tomorrow comes.

THANK YOU

Thank you for being there
When no one else even cared.
Thank you for brightening
My darkest days,
When there was sadness
And grey in the haze.
Thank you for understanding
When I'm grumpy, vexed
And feeling so blue.
Thank you for all those special things
That you say and do.
Thank you for showing me
The things that I could not see,
But especially, most of all,
Thank you for loving me.

PARTS OF ME

There's a part of me
That still likes you.
There's a part of me
That still wants to kiss you.
There's a part of me
That I wish I could see you.
There's a part of me
That still misses you.
The other parts of me
They carry on living.

IN DREAMS

In dreams
We go to a different world,
Where anything is possible
And jumbled-up pictures
Flicker from a kaleidoscope of colours
To shades of black and white.
In dreams
Things can be so true and right.
In dreams
We have extended variations
Of our already complicated lives.
In dreams
I see you, Nan,
With all your little cats
Circling around you and meowing
As loud as they can.
In dreams I see you, Cleo,
My lovely black cat,
Sitting beside me
On the little garden mat.
In dreams
I see you, Dad,
Standing by the pier,
Looking out to the sea
With your fishing rods
And smiling at me.

In dreams
We have no say or control
For a sad or happy end to unfold.
There are no corners
And there are no bends,
And when we awake from our dreams
We are transported back
Into our other real world
With mostly no memories
Of where we've just been to hold
Just a fleeting moment
Of some familiar feeling and time
That brings a tear to our eye
And a little smile.

TIME FLIES BY

Time flies by
As quick as day
Turns to night,
The seasons flowing
Into one another,
The sun rising and falling –
Our celestial mother.
Time waits for nothing and no one –
That big clock in the sky.
Times you've looked forward to,
Times you've put off.
The days – they're just
Not long enough.
You look back
Over your shoulder
And see yourself and the world
Another year older.

WHERE ANGELS SIT

Angels sit on the floor
And on top of a door;
They sit by a picture frame
Near a lit candle
And watch the flicker
Of the flame;
They sit in the garden
And over the hill;
They even sit on the window sill.
Angels sometimes sit on clouds
When things get too noisy and loud;
They sometimes sit on your shoulders
And follow you around
To watch over you
And keep you safe and sound.

NOW THAT YOU'RE GONE

What do I do
Now that you're gone?
How do I sing
My favourite songs?
How do I sleep?
It doesn't work counting sheep.
All my tears and sadness –
When will it end
And there be gladness?
When will I laugh
And smile again?
I've no love left for another –
I gave every drop to you.
There's no regrets though –
I'm still glad I knew you.
Is it true what they say,
That time heals and life goes on
And somehow I'll get through
The days ahead
Even though they may feel long?
I will always miss you
And never forget
Those precious moments in time
When I was yours
And you were mine.
Our days were magical,
Full of colour, happiness and glee
When we were together,
Just you and me.

IT'S ONLY LITTLE OLD ME

If you see a shadow in the distance,
Don't worry, it's only little old me.
If you should hear the swing in the garden squeak,
Don't be scared, it's only little old me.
If you hear a whisper in the wind
And feel something touch your face,
Don't cry, it's only little old me.
If you feel a sudden warmth beside you,
Don't run away, it's only little old me.
And if you smell a heavenly flowery smell,
Be happy as it's only little old me.

THE HAIR SHOP

The Hair Shop
It stands in between
A row of little shops.
Inside it looks lovely –
Clean and so pristine.
The lady that owns it,
A tall, slim, pretty lady
Called Jackie,
And all the other ladies
That work there,
So friendly with panache and flair.
It's the place to be
If you want a pick-me-up and go.
There's lots of regular clients –
You're sure to see someone you know.
Wash, cut and blow-dry,
Colours, foils or a complete restyle –
It's just so nice to sit,
Chat and rest awhile.
You even get a nice cup of coffee
And magazines to read
With all the latest gossip.
You'll feel wonderful,
Pampered and special,
So make an appointment
At The Hair Shop soon.
A warm welcome awaits you –
There's no doom or gloom.
The ladies there
Are so good, true and kind –
Not only will they do your hair,
They'll soothe your soul and mind.

FOREVER FRIENDS

Janet, a gentle
And quietly spoken lady,
Gorgeous manicured nails,
She never flies
Off the rails.
Always a good girl
And stays out of trouble,
No one could ever
Burst her bubble.
And Jan, with her
Lovely warm smile
And cheeky face,
Every now and then
She likes to chase
Half-naked waiters
All over the place.
Then there's Belinda,
With the most beautiful
Water-green eyes –
She'll tell you
All the latest gossip,
Not forgetting the
Nice Russian man
Who's possibly a spy,
A twinkle in her eye.
There's Rebecca,
With her naughty infectious laugh

And lovely golden hair,
So friendly, loving
And with so much panache and flair.
Last of all, me,
With my big brown eyes
And my face all aglow,
Joining in with all the laughter,
Savouring the funny
And interesting stories
That seem to ever flow.
The time that passes
From year to year –
It matters not as
Forever friends
We will always be.

I REMEMBER

I remember long ago
When I was just
A little girl
The summers were warmer
And Mum would make Ribena lollies
And let me play
With my posh lacy brolly.
In winter, when the snow came,
Sledging, snowball fights and silly games.
A huge snowman stood on the green
Made by some children
That lived down the lane.
I remember long ago
When I had to be in bed by eight
Or else next day there'd be no treats
Like home-made cake.
I remember long ago
When school holidays
Seemed to last forever
And I could stay up late,
Watch TV and try on
Mum's nice shoes and make-up.
I remember long ago
If you had a penny
You'd run to the corner shop to spend it
Then skip back home with a silly hum,

A little white paper bag
Filled with multicoloured sweets
Rustling in your hands.
I remember long ago
If you heard the ice-cream van
Coming down the road
You'd rush out and wait for it
On the tips of your toes,
And the fizzy-pop man
Selling gem-coloured drinks
From his little van.
I remember long ago
Going to Grandma's for tea with Mum and Dad –
There were always lovely treats to be had.
I remember long ago
When the days were long
And life seemed slow.
I'm much older now,
And when I'm all alone
And look out of the window
I daydream and wonder
Where on earth
Did all the time go!

MY BUBBLY BATH

Every evening I take
A bubbly bath,
Read my favourite book
And have a laugh.
I see through the round-shaped window
The frosty winter sky.
We're joined at the hip now,
My bubbly bath and I.
There's shimmering bubbles
And rose-scented confetti,
Soothing bath salts
And a bath-bomb smelly.
I'll give myself a pep talk
And put the world to right –
I wish I could wallow
In this bubbly bath all night.

THE NIGHT SKY

Velvet midnight blue,
A blanket of twinkly stars,
Some so far away,
Only a fuzzy hue –
A milky cloud
Of other worlds and wonders.
We stand still
And look up to ponder.
We gaze at the moon,
Looming high in the night sky,
And admire its presence,
A ball so crystal-like,
Gems of yellows, reds and greens.
We pick out the planets
And little streaks of comets,
Spirals of galaxies,
Strings of white pearls
And zodiac constellations
Of wondrous worlds.
The silence of the night sky,
A calmness through the sphere,
The beauty of the night sky
So heavenly and clear.

AUTUMN DAYS

There's something special
In the autumn glow
With the sun in the sky
So orange and low.
Falling leaves,
The colours of fire and amber.
Spun sugar treacle and toffee,
Swirls of chocolate and caramel
In your coffee.
Curled-up leaves
Like little brandy-snap wafers
Skipping around the garden,
Making musical sounds like
Little bits of tissue paper.
The little Autumn Fairy,
She's been so very busy
Spinning all her pretty colours
Into the final picture
That makes autumn days
A truly magical place.

READY FOR WINTER

Time to get ready for winter.
In the wardrobe put away
All your pretty dresses and summer hats
And bring out all your
Blacks, greys and navy slacks.
It's time to rearrange your cashmere cardies,
Bright colours put to sleep,
Making room for the more
Muted colours to peep.
Your gorgeous high heels
Put into shoeboxes
And take out your
Suede and fluffy boots –
You know you always feel so foxy –
And your heavenly faux-fur coat
That always floats your boat.
And say farewell to summer
For another year,
And hello to winter
With all its beauty and cheer.

A WINTER'S DAY

A sprinkling of fresh snow
Glistening under the winter sun's glow –
Wrapped in winter coat, scarf and woolly hat
I stand and stare
At the white fields of frozen air,
All the trees' branches so bare.
A long-eared hare
Watching intently over there,
A little robin hops in and out of a holly bush,
The tiny red berries oh so lush.
In the distance swirls of smoke
Float up into the cold sky
From a chimney pot
On top of a snow-covered house.
A quietness and stillness
Surrounds this fairy-tale white world.
Dotted about in the crystal-like snow,
Little green leaves of snowdrops are starting to show
And buds on bushes are beginning to appear –
A gentle reminder that spring
Will soon be here.

WAITING FOR A SNOWFLAKE

In my winter garden
With my arm held out,
There I stand
Waiting for a snowflake
To softly fall
On to my hand.
I stare at the cold inky sky
And wait for a snowflake
To land on my eyelash
And gently melt into my eye.
I wait for the snowflakes
To sprinkle themselves on to
My curly black hair
And embellish my long fur coat
In snow crystals everywhere
So I can turn into a snow princess.
And with my twinkling snow-covered hands
I magic myself to a faraway
White fairy-tale land.

LITTLE POLAR BEAR

Little polar bear,
Playing in the sparkling snow
Without a care,
Wish I could play rough and tumble
And give you a cuddle.
But I must only admire you from afar
So as not to upset your beautiful ma –
Her pride and joy,
Her only little baby boy
So precious and fragile.
I love your little white furry face
And all your funny tricks and grace.
I love your little shiny black eyes and nose
And how you sit and pose.
Your little white furry legs disappear
As you bounce around in the frozen air
And plunge into the deep snow.
You really put on a magical show,
But when the snow is all gone
Where will you go?
Where will you live?
Will you be safe
And find a new place?
I must promise to lend a helping hand
And protect you and your beautiful white frozen land,
For if you were to be gone
We would cry and miss you
And sing a really sad song
Because we so love you,
Polar bear, little one.

THE LITTLE CHRISTMAS TREE

The little Christmas tree
It stands to attention in a corner,
Its little green branches
Proudly stretching out,
Its feet in a little green pot,
A red skirt of tissue paper,
A golden bow of ribbon.
Adorned with fairy lights,
Charms and trinkets,
It shimmers and sparkles,
Jingles and quivers.
An angel crowns its top
And she bows and curtsies
As she blows golden kisses
And Christmas wishes.
If the little Christmas tree could speak
It would cry out loud with glee,
"Look at me! Look at me!
I'm the most beautifullest
Of all Christmas trees.
Oh, and please don't forget to water me!"
Carefully placed presents
Circle the little tree.
Guardian of Christmas spirit,
You've cast your magical spell on me.
How I love you,
Little Christmas tree.